MAKING LOVE TO ROGET'S WIFE

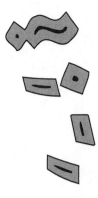

MAKING LOVE TO ROGET'S WIFE

POEMS NEW AND SELECTED
RON KOERTGE

THE UNIVERSITY OF
ARKANSAS PRESS
FAYETTEVILLE   1997

ISBN: 978-1-55728-462-4 (cloth)
ISBN: 978-1-55728-461-7 (paper)
eISBN: 978-1-61075-257-2

25 24 23 22 21   5 4 3 2

Designed by Alice Gail Carter

♾ The paper used in this publication meets the minimum requirements
of the American National Standard for Permanence of Paper for Printed
Library Materials   Z39.48-1984.

Library of Congress Cataloging-in-Publication Data
    Koertge, Ronald
      Making love to Roget's wife : poems new and selected / Ron Koertge.
          p.   cm.
        ISBN 1-55728-462-8 (cloth : alk. paper). —
        ISBN 1-55728-461-X (paper : alk. paper)
        I. Title
    PS3561.0347M3   1997
    811'.54—dc20   96-33030
                                                CIP

for Steve Kowit and Charles H. Webb

ACKNOWLEDGMENTS

Some of the poems in this volume were first published, often in different versions, in the following books and magazines. Thanks to everyone for everything.

Cheap Thrills, Wormwood Review Press, 1976; *Diary Cows,* Little Caesar Press, 1981; *The Father Poems,* Sumac Press, 1973; *Fresh Meat,* Kenmore Press, 1981; *High School Dirty Poems,* Red Wind Press, 1991; *The Hired Nose,* Mag Press, 1974; *How to Live on Five Dollars a Week,* VPC Press, 1977; *The Jockey Poems,* Maelstrom Press, 1980; *Life on the Edge of the Continent,* University of Arkansas Press, 1982; *Men Under Fire,* Duck Down Press, 1976; *Sex Object,* Little Caesar Press, 1979; *12 Photographs of Yellowstone,* Red Hill Press, 1976

Aldebran Review, Apalachee Quarterly, Asylum, Bachy, Bakunin, Bandicoot, Barney, B City, Bear, Beloit Poetry Journal, Beyond Baroque, Big Moon, Blind Alley, Blue Window, California State Poetry Quarterly, Caryatid, Cedar Rock, Chiron Review, College English Journal, Contemporary Quarterly, Corduroy, CQ, Electrum, Erratica, Esquire, The Falcon, Fireweed, 5 AM, Follies, Forehead, Galley Sail Review, Happiness Holding Tank, Herman Review, Hiram Poetry Review, Instant Classics, Invisible City, Italia America, Jacaranda Review, Kansas Quarterly, Linden Lane, Little Caesar, Lodestar, Longhouse, Madrona, Maelstrom Review, Mag, Mandala, Marilyn, The Midatlantic Review, Momentum, Mosaic, Nausea, New Collage, Newletters, New Mexico Humanities Review, Occident, Oh Zone, Oink, Onthebus, The Orchard, Overflow, The Periodical of Art in Nebraska, Poetry/LA, Poetry Now, Practices of the Wind, Purr, Pyramid, Rhino, Road/House, Sausalito Belvedere Gazette, Scree, Second Coming, Smudge, Squeezebox, Stairway to the Stars, Stone Drum, Sumac, Sunset Palms Hotel, Sycamore, Telephone, Tequila Press Poetry Review, Three Rivers Poetry Journal, Trace, Truly Fine Press, Tsunami, Urthkin, Vagabond, West Coast Poetry Review, Western Humanities Review, Whetstone, Wind, The Wormwood Review, Yellow Brick Road

I am also grateful to the National Endowment for the Arts for a 1990 fellowship and the California Arts Council for a 1993 grant.

CONTENTS

NEW

SELECTED

The Art of Poetry

My daughter seems to be freezing.
No one knows why, but the tests
run into thousands.

Her teacher brought a book "so she could
keep up," and while it snows outside
St. Luke's, I'm paging

through. At chapter 8 ("Weather")
I can hear the siren of a poem
in the distance.

It has to do with this cake-colored child,
the numbness of her hands, a drifting
skiff of a bed.

Staring down, clutching my lucky
Bic, I hardly know what to pray
for next.

What She Wanted

was my bones. As I gave them
to her one at a time, she put
them in a bag from Saks.

As long as I didn't hesitate,
she collected scapula
and vertebrae with a smile.

If I grew reluctant, she pouted.
Then I would come across
with rib cage or pelvis.

Eventually I lay in a puddle
at her feet, only the boneless
penis waving like an anemone.

"Look at yourself," she said.
"You're disgusting."

Loving Ugly

On a certain part of lawn outside
the college at the edge of town,
the common student comes to love.

You never see any campus queens
out there or the pouty-looking
owners of Corvettes,

only the underachievers, the ones
who take the bus everywhere
and live at home.

Between classes they lie in the sun,
carbuncle to carbuncle, glasses
folded away, bad breath mingling
like a successful experiment
in Chem. 4B,

while twenty miles away, on the shore
of the blue Pacific, the head cheerleader
and secretary of the freshman class

pulls her short skirt back into place
and says, "Not here, Tom.
Not now."

Ozzie Nelson Dead of Cancer

The Adventures of Ozzie and Harriet were bland
as sleep. Ozzie needed a new tie. Ozzie had eaten
too much down at the malt shop. Harriet wanted
a light bulb from upstairs. David and Ricky argued
over a ball, their voices soft as sheets.

Theirs was a home without a toilet, bills, or tears.
There, no one masturbated or was afraid of God.
No one yelled or crushed things. They ate and slept,
rising in perfect order to greet that day's dilemma
no larger than a dot.

Now, what a loss, Mr. Nelson, Ozzie of Ozzies, perfect
husband and father.

This poem of admiration, black upon white like alien
hands in truce, comes too late as it did for my own
father, as different from you as lamb's wool
is from flesh.

But now, I miss you both.

Admission Requirements
of U. S. and Canadian Dental Schools

Is your furniture in mint condition?
Has the loathing settled down?
Do you have many commemorative coins?
Do you know what the lighthouse stands for
in poetry?
Do you regard "uppers" and "lowers" as versions
of the class struggle?
If you could snow, would you?
Could you wear a red hunting shirt rather than
the traditional white smock?
When someone murmurs, "But my first love
is the oboe," are you disheartened?
If you were a bird, what would be your wingspan?
If someone said his gums were clandestine, would
you look forward to the drilling?
Do you know what makes bipeds wild with joy?
Could you be specific?

Soothing the Unheralded Organs

I understand why all of you would like to be
the Penis, who is treated so gently, has a life
of renown, and is rewarded like an only child
who sings, too.

Just remember that the Penis is not so highly
regarded when he sulks, and he is silly indeed
upon emerging from cold water as collapsed
as a tiny spyglasss.

Praise, then, to the Esophagus: what a good job
you do, easing every meal into position. Without
you, other unheralded organs would be hampered
by steaks and chops. In fact, everything would be
knee deep in water like a flooded basement.

Stomach, I know that you would like to work
outside for awhile, slung across me like an
aficionado's bota. I know you would secretly
like to be as public as the Arms and Legs.
But without you, they would dwindle to strings.
They are aware of this, and Hands at this very
moment are holding something special for you.

Old Liver, surely you do not feel left out.
I give you alcohol rubs every evening.

And Intestines both Large and Small,
you are so sweet about a job not highly
prized in this world. Yet you and I know
what a good time we have.

All the Outsides, from Head to Feet, want
to thank you for laboring as you do in such

darkness. With what good will and alacrity
you have performed all these years.

Best wishes for continued success
from the very bottom of the Heart.

Panty Hose

A little after 5:00, the curb in front
of the Bank of America is rich with typists
holding their cold elbows and waiting
for boys who are pale and hairy, who play
a little guitar and always have some good dope.

These girls in their new panty hose are sowing
every wild oat now because soon they will
leave the hair and the ribs-that-show
for the movie Mom ran every day of their lives.

Already they hate their husbands for sucking
up to big shots, for being first at the polling place,
and for pointing out creeps in vans. They will
never love anybody like they do the one who
is always late. They will never look up and down
the street as eagerly as they do today, not even
when dinner is ice cold and the man on TV says
that someone in a blue Country Squire has just
been killed in a terrible crash.

Plastic Man, Alone in the Luncheonette, Reaches the Length of the Counter for the Salt

I'm bored. Maybe that's my fault.
I have trouble holding down a job.
Maybe that's my fault, too. I know
this much—the cops don't like me
helping out anymore. And I see their
side of it. They go to night school
and do the leg work, then some noodly
guy steps in and takes the credit.

Women are a problem. Sure, picking up
a handkerchief from a block away has
its charms. And they're curious: I guess
you know about what. But it never lasts.
Maybe because I've got the kind of name
they can't see a Mrs. in front of. Maybe
because they know I could put my arms
around them even when they want to lie
down and I'm outside mowing the lawn.

The bad news is it's been downhill for
quite a while now. The good news? If I
ever hit bottom, I'll bounce. But seriously,
folks, I've got a standing offer with the circus:
the Fat Lady and me and a world's
record for the embrace. Or delivering
for any florist without leaving the shop.
Or this waitress right here, her lost
beauty, her eyes wondering if these arms
these fingers could find it for her.

Beautiful Eyes for a Boy

We were a hundred miles from anywhere
as my grandmother smoothed the oilcloth,
rattled the wood stove, sniffed at the ground
round, her daughters, their husbands clustered
on the porch methodically kicking the yard
dog away from their good pants.

I took the Sears catalog and climbed to
the loft of the rickety barn. I knew
the women in Foundations wanted the men
in Briefs and nothing could stop them from
meeting in Comforters & Quilts and kissing
until their blood hissed like broth.

      • • •

Afterwards, dreamy in the straw, I heard
someone yell for me, then lean on the horn
of the Buick I would never be old enough
to drive. I knew the ride home like the palm
of my hand: all two-lane blacktop with white
crosses where high school seniors hadn't
made the curve.

"In a minute!" I yelled. And just before I climbed
down, I thought that I could set the whole place
on fire just by looking a certain way.

The Manager of the Drive-In Dairy

is dressed for the cold, so he might be lecturing
his carry-out boy on the dangers of drafts
and the short-sleeved shirt. Unfortunately,

he is saying, "I like your work, Mark. Really.
But you're not the manager here. I am."

He spots my Dodge, quiet as a cop's, then tugs
the boy into the cooler. I can see them leaning
on the cheese like tired Swedes.

Then the kid drags himself toward my car—a Volga
milkman. "You don't have to take that crap," I say.

"Aw, it's not so bad. And, anyway, another couple
months and I make assistant manager." He points
to his chest. "I get to wear a thing that says so."

I drive home shaking my head, blessing my parents
who never expected me to amount to anything.

Secrets of Writing Revealed at Last

—FOR BILLY COLLINS

It was raining at the race track. I sat
in the parking lot waiting for the eighth,
tinkering with a poem, and reading Henry
James. The heater whispered like the skirts
of his heroines, and those sentences still
measured by the furlong.

I picked up the poem again (it turned out
to be this one), but it was still reserved,
so I just watched the stands exhale nine
thousands fans, each in his new, free, yellow
hat—a host of golden daffodils.

In the back seat Mr. Wordsworth introduced
himself to Mr. James as I played it cool,
just turning the beautiful, orchestrated pages
of my racing form. Then they said in unison,
"Look, Ronald, we have a hunch about #6,
Past Masters. So why not just borrow some
lines from one of your friends. We all did,
dear boy."

I checked my program. Past Masters was 40 to 1.
"Billy wouldn't mind," I said dashing for the
windows.

And that is why my family
today
is so enormously wealthy.

Things That Make You So Scared You Can't Swallow
So You Start to Cry and You Tell
Them That You'll Do Anything
If They'll Just Leave
You Alone

Three thousand down at Hollypark and into the book
for two more. Some strangers are standing by your
car, so you start to hitchhike the other way, but they
pick you up and turn down a dark street.

Spread-eagled in New Mexico: an arena of lights
from eight Chevrolets with angel-hair upholstery.
The long blonde beard you were so proud of is
already gone. Your balls are next.

Up against the wall in East St. Louis. Half a dozen
old diddley-bops with key chains down to their
knees, talking so much shit even they can't
understand each other. One of them cuts
a button off your shirt with a pearl-handled shiv.

Your wife comes out of the kitchen wiping her hands
on a pink tea towel. "It's perfect," she says. "I'm
making a good dinner, you're having a drink, the baby
is playing so sweet. I can't think of anything nicer."

A Dazed Survivor Recounts the Events
Leading Up to the Tragedy

We were calmly
on fire
when some fool
shouted,
"Movies! Movies!"
Then we all dashed
madly
for the center
of the theater.

Christmas Card

Outside the locker room this morning I heard
some guy say into the phone, "But, Jesus, I'd do
anything for you."

I suspect he wasn't talking to The Source,
more likely to a woman in El Sereno taking off
her uniform and name tag and staring at the tree.

Now carols over the loudspeaker make me
wonder if Jesus is looking down at my Speedos
no bigger than a crucifixion panty.

I'm surprised You aren't fed up to here with us.
After all, what do we say except, "I want a pony!"
Never, "Thanks for that tie and the salad tongs."

Well, here's a little something for Your birthday.
This last lap—as hard and as fast as I can—
is for You.

Moving Day

While sitting home one night, I hear burglars fiddling
with the lock. This is what I've been waiting for!

I run around to the back and open the door, invite
them in, and pour some drinks. I tell them to relax,
and I help them off with shoes and masks.

In a little while we are fast friends, and after a dozen
toasts to J. Edgar Hoover, they begin to carry things out.
I point to the hidden silver, hold the door as they
wrestle with the bed, and generally make myself useful.

When they get the truck loaded and come back inside
for one last brandy, I get the drop on them. Using Spike's
gun, I shoot them both and imprint Blackie's
prints on the handle.

Then I get in the van and drive away,
a happy man.

To Impress the Girl Next Door

I go everywhere underground. It is a burden
I prefer because I want to deserve her love.

Accordingly when she goes out, I begin to dig.
The tap of her heels on the pavement drives me on.

Occasionally I come to the surface beside the gas
station. She never even nods, which is as it should

be since she does not know who I am or that, for her,
I live to burrow or how at night, curled in my present

tunnel, I think about her pretty feet and giggle
in the rooty air and go to sleep.

Guys at the Races

I have never seen them anywhere
except the track, so it is hard to imagine
their navels or the backs of their knees
much less their wives—mysterious figures
like the night nurse.

What if they are mean, read little books,
and have birds in the living room.
Do they ever lean, their lifelines
pressed to their brows?

I do, and so what. I like to sit
with the guys, tell a rotten joke,
and talk about the history of this Bold Ruler
until he emerges from our separate minds
not merely favored, but completely loved.

Future Farmers of America

The girls are my favorites,
naturally, their tight white jeans
and rough hands, cute as all
get out with those long poles
for humiliating cattle, their
roper's boots edged in cow shit.

The boys look like tough little
mothers—sleeves rolled up,
belt buckles big as relish trays,
ominous mushroom-shaped laughs:
the kind of kid I was afraid of
in 6th grade on my way home from
school, another A essay riding inside
my Percy Shelley lunchbox.

What a Varied Place the World Is
So Trusting and Strange
So Deserving of Love and Praise

It was wonderful to hear the room
almost go out and then, at the prices,
flare again. It was wonderful all day,
from all 11 tracks, all 99 races, all 900
horses brown, bay, black, roan—
money and numbers til the stars blur.

Half a mile away someone yawns,
breathes his coffee breath in one long
hiss, mounts the catwalk, and begins
to inscribe the names from Saratoga.

Today, too, I will walk into that room
already hot as laundry and feel the voltage
of men who dressed without women, men
who sit all day reluctant to leave even to pee,
perfect in repose, perfect on the verge,
always ready to rise and dance like mad.

Victims

My son is out on the walk just behind
the house. He is stalking ants with a magnifying
glass. I can see him from the kitchen

as he spotlights one for immortality.
Poe-style, he cranks the light to a point,
and the star of the show is fried.

Last night I explained the consequences:
how Momma and Poppa wait anxiously
for their industrious little tyke, how they
finally call the Ant Patrol and get the news
that breaks their black little hearts.

It seemed to excite him: The Sneakered God
Who Kills with a Glance.

Now when he sees me watching, he eyes the ground
and starts for parts unknown.

As he moves, he swims in the window's flawed glass.

Orphan

Other sons had to fly toward cold
airports where mothers waited
covered with tears like pearls
on a show saddle.

Or they had to walk down halls
straight and white as bones,
then watch fathers wired
like homemade bombs.

Other sons could not even shave
without seeing the hair or nose
or chin that was not really theirs.

But the orphan saw only himself.
He had no responsibilities except
to carry his body through the streets
as if it were the Pope's.

He loved his parents for dying
and leaving him alone.

Field Report from Sodom

We believe further exploration
will reveal that all the sweet sins
were named after cities:

Fellatio, always battened down.
Cunnilingus, somewhere
in the tropics. Even little
Onan, with its single citizen.

Lazarus

After Jesus raised him from the dead
and everyone was impressed, He went on
His way while Lazarus stayed home with Mary
and Martha who put together a little party,
just family and friends, but nice, with plenty
of wine and colored lanterns in the trees.

"Don't shake hands," advised one guest,
"he's colder than a well-digger's ass."
"Lazarus is pale as hell," whispered Uncle Enoch.
A niece added, "Lazarus stinks."

Pretty soon they had him sitting nine yards
away from the table, wrapped in a blanket,
discreetly downwind.

Finally he moved back to the tomb,
going out only in the evening to follow
the sun into the West,

God's name in vain on his cracked and loamy lips.

Mr. Big

Every palooka in every B
movie wanted to see him.

And no wonder. Who doesn't
have a problem that only
Mr. Big can solve?

So we sit, turning our gray
hats in our hands.

But it's worth the wait because
any time now he might
come out of that back room

smoking the entire state of Florida.

Killing Time

Fine.

But stop driving it around
in a van first. Stop biting
your nails and sweating,
and for God's sake stop
saying not to be afraid.

Just get it over with.

I Never Touch My Penis

I was taught that touching it is nasty, and
I never do. I have tongs made to hold it

so that I will never do anything nasty
and call attention to myself in some public

place. Next to doing something nasty,
being stared at is one of my greatest fears.

I use the tongs when I go out to a symphony
or a stock car race. My newest pair

is gold and plays "Getting To Know You"
when the tips meet. People did stare

a little when I used my new tongs, but
I think it was just envy on their part

and chagrin at their own flagrant nastiness.

On the Anniversary of His Death the Men of the Village Meet to Talk about Frankenstein

The way he was sewn together
made their skin feel so smooth.
His green-cheese complexion
and stupid haircut made them
look attractive and fashionable.

They didn't have to borrow
some stiff's heart. And they
had real souls, too, not just
fistfuls of bad weather.

Hey, remember the torches
and clubs? Remember running
around half-nuts all night?
And then it was so great to come
home: a bubbling tureen of soup,
wolfsbane on the mantle, garlic
over the door, those grateful wives
who never looked as good before
or since.

"The Thing Is to Not Let Go of the Vine"

—JOHNNY WEISSMULLER

Of course he is right; otherwise, he would not
be Tarzan King of the Jungle, but Tarzan
King of the Emergency Ward.

So as advice goes, it's better than most.
But what happens when Simba and Tantor
grow immune to yodels and he has to face
the evil white men alone? What happens
when Jane's little bark skirts are no longer
fetching, or when he's so tired that the trees
seem taller and every vine's a python?

Perhaps there comes a time at the edge
of some sinister veldt when the thing to do
is not hold on but let go at the peak and fly
into the arms of the Ape Mother at whose
dark and leathery breast we rest, content
at last knowing what it is we have been
all this time hurrying through the forest toward.

Diary Cows

Got up early, waited for the farmer.
Hooked us all up to the machines as usual.
Typical trip to the pasture, typical
afternoon grazing and ruminating.
About 5:00 back to the barn. What
a relief! Listened to the radio during
dinner. Lights out at 7:00.
More tomorrow.

Touring the Crèches

All the Marys were fine, all with those
innocent necks, but Sondra Knott had the eyes,
too, and got my vote. The Presbyterians
used a real baby and Willoughby's donkey,
even though Sonia Willoughby was a Baptist!
The heavenly hosts were pretty good
but mighty low to the ground, and Skipper
Webb, the Unitarian minister's boy,
threw up on all those Glorias.

Driving by again drunk at 1:00 A.M.
on the streets' long rails of moonlight,
all the Magi were home, their beards laid out
neatly on the chifferobes; Sondra Knott asleep
in her sweatshirt and panties; the baby
in the wake of Tonka Town. Only Willoughby's
donkey under a single hanging bulb
like he'd just had an absolutely terrific idea,
one that could change the world.

A Word of Prayer
in the Parking Lot of a Mexican Restaurant

In Nogales, I could fall out of La Luna
right into Casa Caliente. In Nogales,
all the girls on Joy St. were named Maria,
and the ride down was hot and curvy.

But hauling back late for work and wives
and scared of clap and God-knows-what,
there were those crosses massed at every
turn where the carnal world was left behind.

Tonight the neon booms Mañana's!
The bartender is named Roy.
It's time to find the car, time to drive
these roads bright as shrines.

Oh, World, if you still love me,
help me hold the wheel again.

The Undead

You only hear about them in the movies:
a servant will mutter, drinks trembling—
or some of the warty villagers
as they eat their root soup.

The pale heroine, of course, says
she isn't afraid of anything: "You all
go on to the Garlic Festival. I'll
be fine here alone. In my nightgown.
With the window open."

Usually it means vampires, those poor
devils in old tuxedos who need a girl
a night like some suburban stud
with his Corvette and Aqua Velva.

Or maybe it means me today.
Not not alive.
Just undead.

Days Off

Often decorated with small resolutions
about the waistline and the lawn,
each is a micro–New Year without
white sales, confetti, or bitter
arguments in the car.

There is no conifer, flag, or covered
dish to commemorate a day off,
no symbol on the calendar except
the numeral in the corner of its
white room.

But everybody knows that the boss
in his big striped buttondown shoes
is berthed at Desk One while you,
needing a shave, are here in this
tiny breathing space,

this hesitant catch at the top of a yawn
magnified into a day, this moment
the photographer loves when at last
everyone, even the baby, is looking
straight ahead and smiling.

With a Million Things to Do,
the Doctor Muses, Anyway

Hidden in the office are my favorite
books: *An Anthology of Pain, My Pal
The Cyst, The Innocence of Germs.*
I love my rubber gloves, my darling
smock, the needles and the drugs.

Oh, God, the beauty of disease, the huge
wet cloud it leaves, and then the scenery
of death: whole families dismantled
in the field, those souls all rustling
like wheat, the driver of the bus
announcing up ahead there is a stop
to rest and eat and, on the right, a view.

Written Almost in the Dark

as we dress to skirt that
arroyo where animals scream
and always it seems the loudest
right where your girlfriend
disappeared. And even now
at the sight of a person or persons
unknown we're glad to turn
and see the corridor of streetlights
that orderly constellation
the kind that pilots need
to guide them home
after they have been alone
in the rubble of the sky
and they come back to this earth
I love and don't pretend
to understand and never want
to leave unless it is with you.

On the Way Home from ICU

It is the kind of motel
where the sign buzzes and the neon girl
in the black Jantzen suit arcing forever toward
the troubled water even smokes a little.

It is 11 bucks and these kids are checking in
at noon. I see them from my car,
quiet as an iron lung. I can almost feel
their breathing and the last dollar
in change, hot and sticky as the quarters
Mother gave him when he was six.

They are sure that sirens will go off
the minute they touch the knob of Cabin 9
and the diving girl will splash at last,
surface and shout their names to everyone.

They go into the office anyway.
She is thinking of her diaphragm, ringing
the edge with goop like a pastry.
He is thinking about the book he read:
the buttons for all that joy.

For My Daughter

She often lies with both hands behind her head
in a San Quentin pose—arms forming a pair
of small, empty wings.

She does not slip from the bath in a loose
robe, affording Follies' glimpses
of rump and thigh. She does lumber by
in a robe of immense dunciness.

Her dates are fixed up or blind
often, like specimens, behind thick glass.
She leaves late, returns before midnight
afraid, perhaps, she will turn into
something worse.

She comes to me and wants to know what to do.
I say I do not know.
She comes to me and wants to know if it will
ever be all right.
I say yes but it will take a long time.

Dirty Post Cards

They are the primers of smut,
Dick and Jane grown up, undressed
and a little overweight.

Measured in the perfect dose
of the rectangle, each is
a flattened canister of desire.

The backs have no addresses
or sentiment besides the mysterious
language of the stain.

No one wishes we were there,
says we are missed or loved.
No one is having a wonderful time.

In fact, the weather—in rooms
as plain as a mailbox—feels
inclement. On the wall

a mirror resembles a frozen lake,
the bed a shattered Alp,
the couple on their hands

and knees could be searching
for something, holding each other
in order to keep warm.

"These Students Couldn't Write
Their Way Out of a Paper Bag."

—ANONYMOUS

I gather groups of freshmen. I distribute
blue books and pens, then unveil the bag
big as a bus.

They rush in and I twist the opening.
There is much unclassified argot and many
contemporary shibboleths but, sure enough,
nobody is writing his way out.

Still, the bag is moving rhythmically.
There are unified, coherent, and adequately
developed moans. Whatever they are doing
has a beginning, middle and end.

"I want to give you all A's!" I shout
as the bag develops an afterglow
and damp spots appear all over the place.

Ganesha

To Hindus, he is the elephant-
headed god. To those who drive
the San Bernadino Freeway,
it is an exit.

Some of the homes are ugly,
perched on tiny plots, one
lonely sunflower with its face
to the wall, a child on the lawn
with a pan, a mailbox driven
into the ground by bad news.

Hindus would not say, "How terrible
you have the face of an elephant."
Rather, "How absolutely wonderful.
What can you teach me that I
need to know?"

Playing Doctor

They were in the shed behind the oak
beyond the back door. "I'll be Mrs. Jones,"
she said, "and I'll come in complaining
about stuff and you'll have to examine me."
He nodded, sat in the broken chair, fingered
the twine around his neck as she began,
"I have pains here, here, and here so I'd
better undress." He pressed the knot
to her small chest, put his hands on her
tummy, tapped one knee. "I find," he said,
rubbing his temples, "inflammation
of the myocardium, enlarged liver,
a badly tipped uterus, and impairment
of motor functions." Her chin began
to quiver. She grabbed her dress and ran
as he opened a chart and began to write
the news that had surprised him, too.

5:00

The kids across the way tell me
what time it is by looking at
the street more furtively to see
if Mom, the Volvo autocrat,

has slid up to the curb unseen
to tap the wheel with lacquered nails
and stare across the caffeine-
colored hood and do the braille

of being put upon. That's when
I know it's time for beer or wine
or both, when food and oxygen
are not enough to help align

the mysteries of day with night
and all its dreams, regrets, and snores.
Thank god, before the sheet's pulled tight
as skin, before my ancestors

drop into bed with me and cry
or criticize my shorts, there's this
hour or so near 5:00 to modify
the creepy day—this armistice.

So once the cars have pulled away
I look inside the dingy fridge.
Beyond the cheese's new toupee
stands enough cold ale to bridge

the kiltered, broken afternoon
and night's combustible cocoon.

On the Origin of Animal Demographics and Communication

The voyage on the Ark—which had looked
so gleeful in the brochures—turned out
to be a nightmare. Becalmed and bored,
the animals copulated and fainted, losing
an entire species when something huge collapsed
on the pregnant Chuckling Nit, leaving her
mate more alone than anything in history.
Two of the doves never came back, and the slap
of Noah's sandals froze everyone.

Eventually the rain stopped. Eventually
Noah opened the door. They were out before
the stink, going as high, as deep and as far
as they could. Some in their blind misery
and fear circled the globe and came up on
the Ark from the other side. That sound
you hear when you are camping out alone
is the one they made then.

If You Lived Here You'd Be Home Now

—A BILLBOARD

If you lived here you'd be home now
and big sea birds would guide the car
into the orchard.

If you lived here you'd be home now
where sadness never comes, stopped
at the gate by armed guards.

If you lived here you'd be home now
where rapture of the deep lasts
forever and the dark is like
a beautiful wife who sits down
at the piano after dinner.

If you lived here you'd be home now
where the children rush in
and they're not bandaged anymore
and there are Mom and Dad
with the stars behind them.

Caesar's Gallic Wars

Because you
were 26 and sat on the desk with your legs
crossed. Because the longing and the envy
in the room were unbearable. Then you
brought along that hangnail of a husband
and just stood there by the school bus.

You with your slides from two summers ago
in Rome: all that greasy hair, a sleazo by
every fountain. We thought you'd been around.
But you weren't different, after all. You weren't
the one we'd be or lay once we left C.H.S.

That's why we stopped studying and wrote
on your quizzes that Julius C. was a fag
and liked sheep. We watched you cry
in class and leave for a long vacation
in the Ozarks.

We broke you like the dry stick you were.

We won.

Searchlights

For some reason we got dressed up—
to be worthy, I suppose, of the new models.
My father was serious, Mother looked
at the upholstery, I got the balloon.
I remember the solemnity of it all, how
I couldn't touch anything but the brochures,
how cool they were to the cheek and brow,
how I imagined the helium at my wrist would
carry me up and away through a million dying
moths, how the searchlights would follow
me—men pointing, women hand-to-mouth,
the other children stiff with envy—and how
the frantic dealer would have to give my
parents a car to soothe them, something
with whitewalls and a radio.

That was what I imagined. What I knew
was that somehow the searchlights had found
and illuminated my life, and growing up meant
my nose would press against the glass a few
inches higher each year until some August
I'd be sitting with some woman and, seeing
the paths of light scissoring the sky, I'd
cover my tired muscles with good clothes
and talk to the salesmen again, even their
hearts puckered from after-shave.

This poem is in praise of searchlights
which for years revolved wildly,
pointing in the direction I knew I should go.

Horses & Cows

Who couldn't pick out the intruder
in the Derby—udder sloshing, a thousand
lengths off the pace, the jockey
so embarrassed he is wearing a mask?

Would any lover claim wild cows couldn't
drag him away? Could Detroit sell anything
with even a million cowpower? What ruler
could touch our hearts by crying, "My kingdom
for a cow"?

And given the choice by a playful god
to return as one or the other, we think
of Trigger and Flicka, not Elsie or Bossy.

Yet horses do not give tasty milk
by the buckets or divide up into roasts
with palsy-walsy names like Chuck.

Cows do not foam at the mouth from nerves
then fall over backwards on their riders.
Instead they stand around endlessly
chewing their food like good children.

Then one considers the grief that beauty
can bring: the illusionary bit of freedom
and that cinch, a narrow stall, scarred
Dutch door, spurs, fat people.

Perhaps there is something to be said,
after all, for a life of less flamboyance,
for the solace of the herd and the regular
eroticism of hired hands.

Sidekicks

They were never handsome and often came
with a hormone imbalance manifested by corpulence,
a yodel of a voice, or ears big as kidneys.

But each was brave. More than once a sidekick
has thrown himself in front of our hero to receive
the bullet or blow meant for that perfect
face and body.

Thankfully heroes never die and leave the sidekick
alone. We would not stand for it. Gabby or Pat,
Poncho or Andy remind us of the part of ourselves
that is painfully eager to please, always wants a hug,
and never gets enough.

Who could go to that funeral and watch the best
of ourselves lowered into the ground while the rest
just sat there, tears pouring off that enormous nose?

Inventions of Troglodytes

The Hunt
>   At first they tried throwing each other
>   at passing beasts, then wisely hit on
>   the idea of disguise. Everyone would dress
>   up as a different animal and blend right in.
>   That night, somebody blew a horn to signal
>   the beginning of the hunt, but everyone just
>   took off his mask and kissed the person next
>   to him, inventing both the party and jealousy.

Medicine Man
>   He didn't know beans about herbs, but he could
>   dance, which was marvelous to the troglodytes
>   who had tons of people still on all fours. Dancing
>   was so entertaining that one man feigned illness
>   just to see some fancy footwork. He was the father
>   of hypochondria.

Storyteller
>   When the lamplight played on rocky walls
>   and everyone was full of big animal, he would
>   tell the same story, the one about how people
>   had come from the mud and had lain around
>   muddy ever since. Then one night he said,
>   "It wasn't always like this . . ." Everyone's
>   eyes grazed him. He had invented the lie
>   and civilization as we know it.

Boy's Life

Someone gave me a subscription for my tenth
birthday, but it was not about my life then, so it
piled up in my room until I had rheumatic fever.

It is an odd disease that affects the heart,
giving it a murmur. I couldn't go outside or play
so I lay in my bed, hands crossed on the Morning Star
quilt, and strained to hear what my heart was saying.

Since anything that thrilled me was taboo,
I began to read *Boy's Life*. Someone was forever
camping out, and things were forever going wrong,
things adults didn't understand.

Being ill had taught me that. What did my parents
know, whispering outside the door, or the doctor
with his greasy machines?

If I was lucky, I would be fine. If not, my heart
and I would stay inside and look out at the dark
and the quivering branches which terrify
Scoutmasters, but not Skippy or Ted.

They just chase that old bear away by banging
on tin plates then modestly slip back
into sleeping bags, knowing every day will
bring a new problem, one they can easily solve.

The Mummy

Maybe she faints because she's scared
and he's horrible. After all, she's wearing
the filmy nightgown all archeologists
slip into after a hard day at the Sphinx,
and he's dressed like a sore thumb,
arms out in the gotcha pose.

But maybe she's just as hot for him.
Maybe he's really just a big present
coming unwrapped and someone to talk to
about intimate things: what other man
could so completely understand the curse?

He's no flirt, either. As he stumbles
toward her, head back like a guy on skates,
there's no glancing around the tomb
for cuter girls. And look how in love
he is! Carrying her everywhere
like a groom who has been waiting
for a thousand years.

Men & Women

When I was five, my mother and father,
Uncle Chris, Aunt Evelyn, and I drove
to the home place near Olney. I stood
in the front seat between the shoulder
pads watching for fires and wild animals.

At Grandmother's house I played outside.
I liked to hear the Savage .22 and see
the fields of blood. I liked to pee
with the men behind the haunted barn.
Their zippers were long as train tracks,
and I wanted my little thing to be big
and wrinkled and sleepy looking like theirs.

Later riding through the dark, I sat between
my mother and her sister so close that
when they talked the feathers on their
hats touched. *Well, not now* she said
he knows he said it does it hurts some
time have you you do he does he wants

I dozed there in a mist of secrets, slipping
from one fragrant lap to another, hearing
underneath the silver fox and gabardine
the hearsay of the real silk.

At home, Daddy carried me inside and everyone
came to watch me sleep. There they stood,
there I lay, surrounded by men and women.

Have You Heard the One about the Soul?

Follow the prow of your iron across
that tear-stained blouse. Doesn't the scarlet
horizon beckon? Observe those scars
from a cruel father. Aren't they shaped
like swift canoes ready to carry you away?

A school bus goes by so quickly who can tell
the boys from the girls. Doesn't that
genderlessness remind you of something before
the ragged edge of a torn theater ticket meant
everything, before that dream of the animal heads
wrung your heart?

And speaking of hearts, listen!
Doesn't your own right now sound like someone
in galoshes walking away from the enormous,
open door of Paradise?

Excerpts from "God's Secret Diary"

Eve has just succumbed to the handsome serpent.
If I say so Myself, I make a good snake. Now she
is about to feel desire. How peculiar to create it
yet be without it, like Thomas Edison in the dark.

   • • •

Now Adam and Eve have really done it! Each gets
an A for contrition, but out they go, anyway. I must
remember to remove the angel with the flaming sword
before Los Angeles appears. Otherwise people will
think this is a car wash.

   • • •

Today I am ambivalent about these particular
manifestations of my Self. It won't be long before
there will be commandments and pathological
introspection. On the other hand, I am a sucker
for sweet talk. Already Eve is a spellbinder.
She is so cute on her knees that I want to answer
all her prayers.

   • • •

It is Saturday night on Earth. A and E are restless,
perhaps dreading Sunday and reminders of what
their shenanigans cost them. Perhaps it is just
the weekend, and they feel obliged to have fun.

   • • •

I can hear anything in any cosmos and beyond,
yet I choose the sound of their troubled hearts.
What a funny God I am.

She

likes big machines. Trains so long
the caboose is just a memory, yellow
Caterpillar tractors that can run over
anything. And she especially likes
those cranes with a big steel ball
that can knock down neighborhoods.

She says if she were an engineer,
she would stop anywhere to let me
on, crush anyone with her tractor
who was even rude, demolish
a landmark so I could see better.

You wouldn't know it to look at her,
to see her eat Thai food or go to
the movies. But some nights the sound
of powerful engines wakes me.

Outside, the streets are empty,
but in the moonlight the building
next door is pale with apprehension.

Not Only Naked Indian Girls and Booze but 10-Point Bucks That Line Up Just Begging to Be Shot and Bass in Shoals So Thick a Man Could Walk across the Water on Their Backs.

1.
Everyone knows the father of our country,
but what about the mother in her early girlhood
with a suitcase no larger than a locksmith's.
Does she not deserve some recognition lost
in the shadows of the recent UFO landing as
out come the stalks of space and everyone glances
just below the neutron belt and says, "Ah,
drinking buddies of the stars."

What chance does she stand against that!
Who was she, anyway, unrecognized then
unrecognized now, lost forever in Father's
insatiable shadow, Father being George,
of course, who lay in his bed whittling
his teeth and thinking about Martha
who was just his wife and not the country's
sacred loins.

2.
Everyone knows the uncle of our country,
but what about the aunt. There are no posters
for her saying AUNT SAMANTHA WANTS YOU, HON.
And her not pointing with an index finger like
an M-16, but holding open both her arms,
calling back to their sand forts and tree houses
all the boys who rushed off to war, catching them
in time and, just like she was dressing someone
for church, firmly stuffing their souls back
into their bodies like breast-pocket handkerchiefs
into a thousand Sunday suits.

3.
The father and the uncle of our country stand
there in the light which if not failing is certainly
getting a D. The loam is over their shoes
and the simple breaths they take affect
the weather map. They are so weird—
that wig, those striped pants. And tall enough
to look out over the world

They like being together. They like being alone
high above the aprons and the smell of fish.
They like to shake hands and pound each other
on the upper arms. If only they had a dog.
The Beast of Fifty States! Then the three of them
could take turns protecting the womenfolk,
all of whom are precious in their sight,
exceptions listed toward the back.

George remembers when he was only a twinkle
in the eye of the limitless grasses, before there
was a map for bullies to copy from the weaker kids.
"Do you remember back then, Sam?"

"Nope, I was always flesh. And before that,
blood."

Night

Lying with you now,
arm numb as a lapel,
I see there could be
anything up there,
not just the bears
and dippers Daddy
traced as he held
us high as groceries.

Look, there's a river
in its dark clothes,
one crushed corsage
the size of Maine,
new kinds of love,
that room we always
wanted to see
but were afraid.

Why didn't someone
tell me that more gods
than I ever imagined
cruise overhead each
night in their enormous
glass-bottomed boat?

Pornography

—FROM *PORNE*, PROSTITUTE + *GRAPHEIN*, TO WRITE

A man turns off Easy Street
and walks in the shadows until
he is greeted: "Hello, Handsome
Sailor, et cetera."

Inside, the man is embarrassed.
"Gee," he says, "I hoped with
a harlot I wouldn't have this problem."

"Catch," she says, tossing him a
Big Chief tablet.

Wow! Things he never dreamed
of. And even better—things
he always dreamed of.

"Say, is there a name for this stuff?"

"Nah," she says fluffing up the red
velour wallpaper. "It's just something
I jotted down."

Green

My mother grew sweet potatoes
in the kitchen window. They loved
her heavy touch and wound
around the knickknacks on the sill.

Her green thumb was famous
and people brought an ailing
coleus or fern from miles away.
She always sighed and said
she would see what she could do.

In grade school I liked a girl named
Deena Vanderwall. Everything
was fine until her mom arrived
one day with a frail African violet.

I saw Deena look for a verandah
and see only sweet potatoes,
oilcloth on the kitchen table,

and my father's boots standing
by the door like tired privates.

Coming Out

of the hospital with the news
that she has a skull like marmalade
and may, at fifteen, learn
to talk like a fish,

I look in the window of the store
by the bus stop and see my
open collar
tousled hair

and I think that in another day
or two, when the smudges
under my eyes are even darker,

I will be very, very attractive
indeed.

The Strain of It All
Drives Bambi Mad

He imagines himself in black leather.
He wants to need a shave and smoke
straights while a tough-looking doll
rubs his antlers.

But the gun in the cabinet shoots only
marshmallows, while kitchen knives
are really woodpeckers who duck
and grin when Bambi tries to stab himself.

He takes off running, Walt's name
in vain stuck in his throat. He flees
across picturesque streams, up lovely
peaks. He runs for hours and never
gets away from primary colors.

He is so tired he could puke, but when
he tries, the daisies only smile and put
their petals over their eyes, embarrassed
to be so close to everybody's darling.

Missing Persons

When Bill and Betty and I began to talk about
them, we meant the fresh-faced choir directors
and assistant pastors caught having affairs,
who vanished into some Protestant Siberia,
the moving van rumbling in at midnight,
and next morning the house was empty
except for sheet music and a shattered lamp.

Where did they go? Downhill, no doubt,
to the deeper South, to churches smaller and smaller,
further and further into the strip-mined hills.

These young men, who still worried about their
complexions, were simply not prepared
for the beauty in those choir robes, or the plight
of young women, married forever, whose husbands
treated them like dirt or, if they were lucky, like dust.

It must have been so exciting, those lips
that pronounced the *o* in *God* like the one in *woe*
whispering into the rectory carpet that he loved
her and everything about her, and knowing, the both
of them, always knowing, that somewhere a van
was idling ready to swoop down and take him away.

We began to joke about sin and how if all of it
in every church was brought to light, it wouldn't
be safe to even cross the street, so dense would be
the trucks. We laughed about men who got out
of the God-business but could never forget the thrill
and had to turn to strange practices, perched
in the cab saying, "Now step on the gas, Sweetheart,
and rev her up. That's what I really like!"

Catholics, we reasoned, were the lucky ones: they understood the near occasion of sin. They confessed constantly and were forgiven. But we were not Catholics and are not now anything at all, something for which I am sometimes heartily sorry.

The History of Poetry

After the fatal snack, Adam felt
so strange that he stayed up late scratching
in the dust with a stick. Then just
before dawn's new appointment
he crouched down and read out loud:

I love being human.
I love having skin and a heart
that beats fast. I love being under
the long, slow tongue of the sun. And you!

No wonder God's big shoulders heave.
No wonder He has turned His face away
from your pretty leaves. You are more
beautiful than He ever was.

Eve was asleep, but the animals weren't,
and they stopped chewing. They had never
heard sounds like that, sounds that made
them pause and blink. Not even in Eden,
not even when he said their names
for the very first time.

Darkness Fell

but did not break, so it is at least as good
as the space-age materials that accompanied
our astronauts to the moon where they gazed
down like God in His infinite boredom
and wondered what their wives were doing.

Unlike darkness, Corning Ware breaks easily.
And when it does, someone usually says,
"You clumsy bitch. Do you think I'm made
out of money?" And someone usually replies,
"I don't think of you at all, you pitiful bastard."

Lord, how this poem is suddenly freighted
with sadness, though it began in the gloaming
and the bare lamplit arms of a cliché
inspired by you in the kitchen weeping
silently into all that broken glass.

Nurses at the Beach

They have seen the great in bed
and know how those dying sweeten
at the end. They chat about the one
who cries for swans, that giant
in Rm. 9, a certain tranced contessa
down the hall, those ponderous wings
that nurses hear, and when they do,
the man who shot the elk is first
to call for help, and then the hero
from Nepal, and last the burning girl.

Right now they wrap themselves in sand.
Gossip trickles from their lips. They mostly
sleep and dream a nurse's dream:
"The Missing Chart & Dr. Small." Except
for Jill who understands the sickness
in the sea and fathoms pain and how
her hands could heal it all, how flesh
could turn to scales, how breasts grow
large and cold, and combing out her
heavy hair upon the rocks, she'd draw
the ships of fervid men to her at last.

Christmas Eve

is also the night the animals can talk.
One would think they'd love it, at first
to praise Jesus, then to speak about
the things they have felt and thought
all year: What is inside the house?
Why do men weep? Isn't it weird
to be meat?

So they hit their marks in the crèche,
see the morsel of divinity, hear
the tortured words. And it is all profoundly
unsettling because the ox is still an ox
in his heavy ox's body, and the donkey's
lips almost bruise making the O's
Hosannahs demand.

Christmas Day is best. The farmer,
a little drunk in his new boots,
has added a handful of grain to the hot
mash, and when the animals bow their
heads, there is the sound of small bells.

Sex Object

She comes home steaming.
She gets into my pants.
She rides me hard.

I look past her slot-
machine eyes
to the ceiling

where the last quake
made cracks in the shape
of Florida

and Louisiana, the latter
having for its capital
Baton Rouge,

which is located
on the Mississippi,
principal waterway
of the United States,

measuring 2,470 miles
from its source
in northern Minnesota
to the Gulf of Mexico.

At Gerlach's

We are waiting outside this liquor store
for the racing form. It is a kind of bliss,
stationed here in the rain, a mammoth score
making tracks in our brains as the hiss
of every van turns the heads in every car.
Then up comes the ragged nail, the bad cigar.

Beside me—his license plate says DUDE—
is a skinny guy, face long as Florida,
reading a thin book about big girls. Next to
him, sunk in the poster for a corrida,
a Hispanic kid wearing one black glove
ignores the Tecate girl who sends her love

to everyone who's ever been alone
with a *TV Guide* spectacled by beer
cans. Wait. This could be the blessed van, bone
white, that sidles nearer, nearer, near.
The paper still retains the presses' heat.
The coming hours tangible and sweet.

Nags

It is not a word I hear much
anymore around the saddling
paddock or in the cool, dim
tunnel that leads to the main

track. But today as a roan
mare limped past, it flew out
of someone's mouth, and I
was nine years old. A cartoon

wife held a rolling pin as her
husband, shoes in hand, swayed
at the foot of the stairs.

Naturally I bet the horse heavy,
and she won by daylight.

Then I could afford Sheila
whose speciality is scorn,
indifference, and an attitude
that would break a lesser man.

Coloring

Here is the handyman with black legs
whistling in spite of gangrene. There
are some smiling cows, red as sores.
A jaundiced mare is chewing peacefully.
Two pea-green farmers chat about nausea.

Cute, but no real grasp of the agricultural
situation. And ending mysteriously
around twelve or thirteen with only
the white crayola intact, used for the silly
sheep, a snowman, or the rare Klan meeting.

And no wonder! Whoever heard of The Nobel
Coloring Prize. Who says, "This is my son.
He has a Ph.D. in Coloring"? Certainly
no one ever grows up and gets a job
in the Arco Plaza—"The Chairman can't see
you now he's coloring can't see you now
he's in a crayon seminar can't see you
now he's about to do the barn."

Perhaps some gland does it. Subdued
by greasier hormones, it atrophies or sleeps
as we crouch at the window on rainy days
every new hair on our new bodies standing
on end as the pillows become the kids
at school we want to kiss or kill as we
move out of childhood outside the lines
into the real where the sun is not a perfect
cookie in the sky but a big hot thing
like us threatening to destroy the world.

The War

When I was a child in the forties, the market
was an island of women, and all they talked about
was love—how they loved their clothes, white
as Jesus' feet, their ironing boards pointing East

like the prows of warships, their children noisy
and huge, the husbands who used to knock two
times on the bedroom door before slipping in.

Oh, there were men around, if you could call them
that: 4F, Sissy, Duck Boy. But nobody who made
women lean against the tilted glass of the meat
counter and order something they couldn't afford.

But I didn't know that then. I was four or five,
weaving in and out of their legs like a tom, gazing
up at the bottoms of their breasts and chins.

I thought their words fell on me like sweet rain,
and all they talked about was love.

All Thumbs

When he
stepped
to the curb,

every car
in the world
pulled over.

Summer Job

There I stood holding the hoe
like a drum major. There they stood,
barehanded, bareheaded, so brown
they were almost cured and each
and every one with something chopped
off, caught in a baler, combine, spreader.
And the more they were missing,
the harder they worked.

"Compensation," I muttered with my B
in Psychology II.

They looked at my hands, dressed like
morons. "As a rule, kid, the weeds
don't grow in rows."

Easter

My wife is standing in the kitchen
saddened by the death of a black
and white cat who took his meals here.
There is a swan on the back of her T-shirt,
and when she tugs it up to wipe one eye,
he lifts off the perfect meter of her beaded belt.

It is the thirteenth Sunday of a short year
and, as I roll away the little stone of my hangover,
I wonder how Jesus felt. He knew how we fumble
for each other's lips, how our thoughts go sneaking
around. Yet He got up, anyway, fussed til the drape
of His sheet was just right, then stepped out
into the lush, blue light of a new day.

The Last Siesta

All summer I have slept with books,
and now Labor Day in its coveralls
has pried open some door, and everyone
is heading home with a souvenir mug

while I grip this mystery and scan
the closing sentence like someone
looking for his keys. I don't want
to say good-bye to the last word

perched at the railing of the novel
and looking back at my rented lawn,
that prince next door, the thin lips
of the sea, the rest of the known world.

Baby, It's You

Poetry lifts language from its knees
in the kitchen, from its tired behind
at a desk full of bills, from off its feet
beside the ironing board, from under
the Nova that needs a clutch.

Poetry kisses with its mouth open
and whispers, "Sure, I'm idiomatic,
but nobody loves you like I do."

Sweaters

Who can help but love the cotton with its slow
drawl, or the lambs who stand quiet as salt
shakers beneath the shearers' noisy mow,
or even reviled polyester which is nevertheless
visible from a great distance and lasts longer
than most stones.

And my sweater is best of all—almost surely
the model for Michelangelo's "Sistine Sweater"
as well as great-great-grandsweater to the one Emily
Brontë referred to when she said to Charlotte, "How
little he loves me. No sweater in this morning's post."

I wear it all the time except for summer when,
carefully folded as a treasure map, it lies in its cedar
chest studded with moth balls, which are the drug
of choice for sweaters, making them dream of high
winds, bosomy igloos, and the adorable perspiration
of men and women who stand steaming in the half-
light of the first day of fall.

Now and Then

means occasionally
as expressed by the man who takes
a single eggnog near the festooned tree,

but they are wonderful words on their own.
Now being the wall of milk in all that
backed-up light at Vons. Then

the cool schmoo-shaped bottle that every
morning stood sweating on the steps
like a guilty husband.

"Fundamentalist Group Rejects Nudist Campsite"

All those oranges, all that warm wood,
grass mashed the way those nudists do,
the stutter of a nudist still hanging in
moist air, a nudist's glass of milk half-
finished in that dining hall, the air
shaped by nudists, lake made to rise,
the dock nudists dove from in perfect arcs,
the tenderness of nudists, the strange
nudist alphabet, the wounds of nudists
healing, coughing of nudists in the dusk,
the unmade nudist beds, a trumpet hanging
from its peg the nudists' lips upon it, nudist
prayers rising into a bare sky, the stars
burning in the dark like nudists' eyes.

Grace

Vegetables are on their best behavior
in the market, all scrubbed and demure
like kids who have been bussed in
for a dance at the correctional facility.

Fish are slimy but they pucker up a lot,
and everybody knows it's possible for humans
to be so lonely that a fish gets kissed,
sometimes passionately.

Chickens look great with a tan, basking
at the center of any table. And with the way
Dad goes on about breasts and thighs, children
get to see the world in a new way.

So today as I look down at the plate, I want
to thank everything that died for me. Not just
the hops that made this beer or Mr. Lobster
in his cozy thermidor, but the random deaths
the ones that nobody knows anything about.

Trail's End Curios

Outside, the mighty Fahrenheits are beating
against the windows while I'm sitting by
the world's oldest corn dogs which resemble
cattails, an image likely to be filed under
Mojave Humor when my work is catalogued
by supple teaching assistants.

Since I long to be famous and loved by everyone
in the world, I am writing a poem. My fellow
travelers only want to be loved by a few people
and be famous in their bedrooms. So they
turn over the jackalope post card and write
"Wish you were here."

After which they cross the room to a cowboy
painted on the wall and slip the card into his mouth,
which is frayed like he has been sucking cactus.
Then they turn looking satisfied and pleased,
the way I look as I close my notebook on another
poem destined to make everyone who reads it
happy to be alive or, if they fold it and stuff
it in one shoe, a little taller.

NEW !

My Name

In the old days, you were
what you did: Baker,
Cooper, Shoemaker.
And a sign saying so hung
on creaky chains above
a whitewashed door.

What about me back then
with my nearly
unpronounceable name
which sounds like Cur
Cheese—a dairy product
from snarling dogs?

There I'd stand under my
bewildering sign while
the maidens passed arm
in arm with Mr. Cook, Mr.
Archer, Mr. Golden Pants.

Out of Body Experiences

At first it's not much different from being
separated from the class on a field trip,

and it's fun to look down from the cream
ceiling and see the big bruised body.

So will it be God's laser light-show,
or the hedge of yawning relatives?

Everything gets to vote: shapely brain,
cowering genitals, deep branch of ulna,

palatine canal, glands of Bowman,
the scars, the sweat. And time after time

we choose the light rungs and descend
willingly to enter the blossoming flesh.

Thirteenth Birthday Party

"What a special night!" they cried.

"A rite of passage," said my aunt,
the voluminous reader.

The men winked at me. The women
pulled their skin tight. "Oh, to be that
again," they said into the cracked

mirror of the coffee table which,
in two more payments, would belong
to my parents.

The Other Side

It is almost always somewhere
else. In Heaven, for example, where
the freight yards are spotless, no one
needs calcium supplements, and
everybody is happy, especially
the philosophers counting angels
on the tiny dance floor.

But sometimes it is not that far,
and we mean only the cooler side
of the pillow, a sunny street,
Ted's side of the story, or the famous
fence beyond which stands no Lawn
Boy or Bandini, but a heart-breakingly
beautiful meadow with a path
that leads everywhere.

And every now and then we are happy
right here: a perfectly acceptable
bed, mist on our new yellow boots,
that novel we have been saving,
our own lawn running all the way
to the French doors like someone
returning from exile.

Ruidoso, N. M.

We have come through the suburbs
of the moon to these mountains
drawn on a map in hurried lambdas,
like the work of a junior cartographer.

But they are beautiful in person,
and I love sitting on the porch of this
motel, the room number over my head
so I resemble Euclid on vacation.

I am pouring over the dark biographies
of horses, counting the money I will
probably not win tomorrow while
the lips of the great American dusk
hover just inches from my own.

A Little Kid

starts whirling around
with his arms out,
and pretty soon

all the kids are doing
it. One girl spins wildly,
and every time she falls

her dress flies way up.
A tall boy eggs another
on until they both puke.

As two girls rush over
with paper towels,
a third goes to

the sandbox and begins
a rehabilitation center
for the famous who will

have trouble with whirling
all their lives.

The Man in the Moon

He seems to have a scar tonight, as if he has been
fighting with sailors attracted or repelled
by his perfectly round head.

He could have two wives, like one of those men
you read about, men who travel a lot.

The sun seems to wound the sky, but not him.

It is Armstrong whom he remembers, Armstrong
tentative and elated like someone
buying a new mattress.

He will never get a passionate phone call
or hear the sighs of the eavesdroppers.

Without a nationality he is, if anything, a Bedouin.

His distant neighbors are stars, robed in red
or white, burning like weightlifters.

It is possible he is not poised up there,
but hanging from a dark noose.

Road Kill

In the parking lot of Wyoming Downs,
bumpers were crusted, grills bent,
headlights shot with blood. And driving
toward St. George, I thought I could see
by the side of every unmown road
the terrible afterglow of the torn.
It made me long for the freeways
with their odd shoes and Kmart
lime-green panties, things which
barely suffer at all compared to
that lynx just outside Salt Lake City
whose ill-timed leap will resonate
to you and me on those nights
we can't sleep, don't want to screw,
and for no reason at all burst into tears.

In Search Of

Every week a new monster,
ghost, or extra-terrestrial:

drawings on a rock, circles
in crops, a cave laced
with scat, a bed too long
for human men, ruins

of a verandah in some
shallows, meteors that
spell, a night-table
that bruises, mist

in the forger's salon,
something in shadows
almost tall, us looking up
our solitude broken. *So,*

we say, *the rumors
were true.*

Making Love to Roget's Wife

We'd meet in a different cheap room.
Every time I had to swear I worked
with horses and used books to kill flies.

But nothing happened until
we heard Peter from the courtyard
below: "Strumpet, demirep, courtesan,
jade, wench! . . ."

Then she closed and barred
the whitewashed shutters
and stepped out of her only dress.

The Lost Continent

No name to write across emerald
maps in a graceful curve, no major
export except mystery. No people
longing for skin lighter or darker
than their own. No cities with the clang
of pastry sheets, smell of eucalyptus,
glitter of trombones.

Since the stranded everywhere
know to send their hopes up a rope
of smoke, maybe that is what
the astronauts saw through their
chilly window: not the flames
of a rain forest, but the Lost Continent
waiting through still another terrible night.

I Take My Toes

completely for granted. In a marriage,
this would call for counseling or at least
a weekend somewhere with a peculiar
bed and wall paper. But this is not
a marriage. These are my toes.

I am only thinking about them now
because the one who wanted roast
beef is broken, and he cannot endure
the tropical ghetto of the Florsheim.

The injured party sits there, mostly
black, beside his yellow neighbor
and their salmon-colored pals looking
for all the world like an ad for UNICEF.

The Kids-Only Motel

It's not that far from school,
and sometimes they just read
their history on the Dumbo quilt.

They usually can't resist, though,
and a phone call to the office
brings someone in a blue apron.

For a price, she will help with
homework. For a price, she will
kiss good night. For a price

she will whisper, "You are
a wonderful child. Unique,
and deeply loved."

Lava Soap

Patient in its little dish, unnerving
in its longevity, this thick ingot
the color of Tijuana jade is still
for men who work hard—
gardeners, butchers, mechanics,
guys who laugh and pass it

along as they get ready to take
down jackets with sneers on the back
and fly across some unnamed lake
toward a woman modeling her skin
like a new dress.

Don't ask how, but I know the Angel
of Death washes with Lava every evening,
then has a hot meal and slips into bed,
both ghastly hands parting the gown
above his wife's quickening heart.

An Infinite Number of Monkeys

After all the Shakespeare, the book
of poems they type is the saddest
in history.

But before they can finish it,
they have to wait for that Someone
who is always

looking to look away. Only then
can they strike the million
keys that spell

humiliation and grief, which are
the great subjects of Monkey
Literature

and not, as some people still
believe, the banana
and the tire.

Hula

When my father came back
with a girl on his forearm,
I asked where she lived.

"Wait til you're older," he said.
"Then I'll tell you."

I went that night.
All the hula girls looked
the same: blue skirt, blue
hair, red nipples and lips.

"The hands," they said wearily,
"don't tell any story you
want to hear, kid. Just watch
our hips like everybody else."

I woke up crying. My parents
loomed over the bed.

"You were dreaming," they said.
Dad hummed "Sweet Leilani."
Mom swayed, her hands
carving up my room.

I watched Dad watch her hips
and hum faster.

Flirting with Poetry

Imagine you are flying cross-country
and beside you in 4E is a beautiful
poem. You sneak a Certs, wish you'd
worn your best sweater and finally
suggest an in-flight beverage.

Soon the tiny stars of reading lights
go out, so you lean closer, pour the last
of the wine and ask what the poem
does for a living.

Effortlessly it sings into your flushed ear
a song you want to hear over and over,
especially through the long heron-glide
to touchdown and the yelp of huge tires.

Waiting in the glare of the terminal
surrounded by your big dumb bags,
you dread the ride home: there's bound
to be a chase, gun shots, a fire.

Silently, you vow to change even as
Prose pulls up in its booming red car
and at the top of its lungs orders you
to keep turning the heavy pages of your life.

First Grade

Until then, every forest
had wolves in it, we thought
it would be fun to wear snowshoes
all the time, and we could talk to water.

So who is this woman with the gray
breath calling out names and pointing
to the little desks we will occupy
for the rest of our lives?

"On the Tip of My Tongue"

There it is again, poised like a diver
about to enter the deep pool of conversation.
Or perhaps hanging on for dear life,
content with the mouth and its white
furniture, not anxious to enter the chilly
world of idea and invective.

Finally I sputter or swear while the word
takes an escalator to the teeming brain
and relaxes in a cozy furrow with his friends,
the other nouns, while some passive verbs
wait shyly behind the leg of the Y in MEMORY.

Boy

He may have been generic,
but his father loved him. When
Boy was kidnapped by cannibals,
Tarzan roused every beast
in the jungle. Knocked on the head
by a coconut, Boy woke to cool
water and a dazzling smile.

That's why I wanted to wear leather
underpants and live in that tree-house,
even though bark gave me hives,
and I had to pee.

From up there I first saw my
father's bald spot, the narrow yoke
of his shoulders. The way he
threw back his head and drank,
he could have seen me, too,
had he opened even one
of his tired eyes.

Books

Rarely as big as the dog door,
they nevertheless drew me
away from a life where someone
cut grass and cherished salt
shakers in the shape of huts.

But it wasn't just being lost
in the snow with a dog,
or exploring dark, beety Russia.
It was also the unblinking page
in my lap and the way words
were separate and didn't seem
to mind that helped me think

those were only boots on the mud
porch, after all. The rooster's gooey
comb could heal, and the size
of the night in the sick room
was what it was.

So when our library burned
and Miss Simmons shrieked
and tore away from the first
fireman, I understood and watched
from across the street in the way
the books had taught me.

The Abstraction Ladder

What with semiotics and deconstructionism,
few teach the Abstraction Ladder anymore.
It hangs in the faculty garage, so to speak,
just above that tarp thrown over the subjunctive.

Anyway, everyone knows it is not Canine
that comes to the rescue; it's Lassie.
And that is not some archetypal Holstein
standing in your field. It is Blossom, decorated
like a map of the Americas.

What no one knows is how glad the abstractions
are to be left alone, their heads happily
in the clouds. Mankind lies around listening
to Music. Opportunity practices his minimalist art.

Only one thing upsets them and that is when
a human ascends each perfectly doweled rung,
a trench coat over his uniform, his name
like a dagger clenched between gleaming teeth,
insisting that he has a date with History.

A Night School Teacher
Looks at His Final Class

At first they were all fidgety
as people in rented tuxedoes.
Their new anthologies cracked
like ice, and they wrote
down everything I said.

Now those geometric rows
resemble the lines ants
make. Answers to questions
we all know the answers to
are accompanied by a languid
hand, the wave of someone
looking for a light cord
in a dark but familiar room.

As usual I like most of them,
but this time there are two
I dream about: Mr. Hancock,
who insists a pacemaker
will remind him only of the
beauty of metrics. And Ms.
Ortiz, legal secretary-to-be,
her wonderful pumps
the color of stallions' blood.

Hermits

They never go shopping for a new hair
shirt or something special for dinner.
They stay in caves looking out at a
monocular world, an imperfect circle
interrupted by a bird or a cloud
resembling the Lamb of God.

The first hermit was probably Paul
of Thebes, the most famous St. Simeon
Stylites on his pillar, the most recent
were Herman's Hermits, a band from the 60s.

Herman himself had thatched hair that
reminded me of something a hermit
might sleep beneath as he traveled
by night, looking for a spot more barren
and unforgiving than the one before.

But that is the only resemblance. They
were just boys who wanted to be famous
as the Beatles. Though in interviews each
said separately that he'd spent many
hours alone in his room looking out
a window where occasionally a bird
flew, by or a cloud resembling a frenzied
girl in the second row on the end.

A Guide to Refreshing Sleep

It is best to remember those nights
when grown-ups were singing and breaking
glass and someone who smelled good
carried you up hushed stairs toward strange
cold bedrooms to be launched on a dark
lake of coats.

If Memory does not suffice, you may
summon the obvious mascots of sleep,
but forego counting. It is miserly. They
will come and stand by your bed, nodding
their graceful Egyptian heads, inviting you

across the crooked stile to one of those
hamlets nestled between blue hills
where the curious are curious about sleep,
the enthralled are enthralled with sleep,
and the great conclusion is always,
"It's time for bed."

Look—a cottage door stands open. On the night
table is a single candle, yellow sheets are turned
back, and in the garden are marshaled
the best dreams in the world. Lie down.
The horrible opera of the day is over.
Close your eyes, so the world which loves you
can go to sleep, too.